First published in this format 2014

All text and photos: Vera Vandenbosch
Jacket/Cover and Interior Design: Kimberly Adis
Executive Editor, Series: Shawna Mullen
Assistant Editor, Series: Timothy Stobierski
Series Art Director: Rosalind Loeb Wanke
Series Production Editor: Lynne Phillips
Series Copy Editor: Barbara Cottingham

The Taunton Press
Inspiration for hands-on living®

The Taunton Press, Inc., 63 South Main Street,
PO Box 5506, Newtown, CT 06470-5506
e-mail: tp@taunton.com

Threads® is a trademark of The Taunton Press, Inc.,
registered in the U.S. Patent and Trademark Office.

The following names/manufacturers appearing in
Bungee Band Bracelets & more are trademarks:
Crafter's Pick™, E6000®, Fabric Fusion®, Hancock
Fabrics℠, Hobby Lobby®, Home Depot®, Jo-Ann®,
Michaels®

Library of Congress Cataloging-in-Publication Data
in progress

ISBN: 978-1-62710-889-8

Printed in the United States of America
10 9 8 7 6 5 4 3 2 1

Contents

Basic Techniques

Cutting and Gluing Cords

When cutting bungee cords, it is important to immediately secure the ends with clear tape or a drop of your favorite glue to prevent fraying. Do this by wrapping the end of the cord with tape before you cut through. Or, immediately after cutting, you can dip the cut end in a dot of glue. There are all sorts of glues available, but jewelry making glue (such as E6000®) or super glue will work well. Handle any glue with care, and follow the package instructions carefully. Fabric glues, such as Fabric Fusion® and Crafter's Pick™ fabric glue, list themselves as nontoxic adhesives, and the list goes on and on—you may want to experiment with your favorite glue on some scraps to see what works best for you.

When cutting very thick nylon cords, it is important to wrap a piece of clear tape around the cord before cutting. You will then cut through the cord and tape together. The tape will hold the fibers together.

Wrapping Cords

Here's a step-by-step tutorial on how to wrap a cord with nylon mason line or embroidery floss. When using mason line, always secure the ends as described above to prevent unraveling.

1. Prepare the cords that need to be wrapped by taping them together with a piece of clear tape. You can even add a small dab of glue for extra security.

2. Cut a length of mason line or floss. Align a one inch length with the area that needs to be wrapped. Start wrapping tightly from right to left, over that one inch piece.

3. Keep wrapping until you have covered the entire area.

4. Cut off the mason line or floss and carefully tuck under the end with a scissor blade. Glue the end of the wrapped area.

Closures

Here are few different types of closures that can be used for bungee bracelets and necklaces.

Bungee hook clasps fit 0.15" bungee elastic cord. The cord easily attaches to both hook and loop with a small drop of glue.

Bungee fashion hooks are very similar to bungee hook clasps, but provide a bigger visual statement.

Two split rings and one key chain clasp are another way of connecting cords together. Depending on the diameter of the split rings, multiple cords can be attached and wrapped.

The **bungee lobster claw closure** allows you to loop a 0.15" bungee cord through one end, and clips onto a loop at the other end. Use the wrapping technique described on the facing page to make the loops.

A **bracelet clasp** is perfect for accommodating thicker ¼" cords OR for inserting a combination of 0.15" cords and parachute cords (as is done for the Bead Bracelet on page 10). A few drops of glue are needed to secure the cords in both ends of the clasp.

A **toggle closure** is the perfect finishing touch for a bracelet or necklace, and can accommodate multiple or thicker cords depending on the diameter of the cups.

Spring coils in combination with a lobster closure are another way to connect cords. Again, the diameter of the coil needs to match the diameter of the cord. You will need a pair of pliers to secure the spring coil in place.

Carabiners come in various sizes, colors and shapes. Here are two examples: (left) double-sided, also called S-biner; (right) single-sided.

Last but not least, the simplest closure of all: a **double knot** at the end of one cord and a loop at the end of the other. This works best with elastic cord, as the loop needs to be able to stretch a bit.

Ball Chain Bracelet

Combining the bright colors of bungee cords and nylon twine with the sparkle of silver or gold ball chains—most commonly used for lighting fixtures or bathroom sinks—gives these bracelets sparkle and personality. In fact, they're quite reminiscent of colorful Indian bangles and they look best when worn in multiples. Fortunately, these are a breeze to make, so you will not want to stop at just one!

To Make Bracelet

SKILL LEVEL
Beginner

CORD
Half a yard of elastic bungee cord 0.15" dia.

Spool of mason line

NOTIONS
Scissors

Glue

Lobster claw clasp 1¼" length

Clear tape

Packet of ball chain

1. Cut a 14½" piece of elastic bungee cord and lightly glue both ends to prevent fraying. Slip one end through the hole of the clasp and fold over by about 1¼". Fold the other end of the cord over, so that both ends are touching. Secure in place with a small dab of glue and a piece of clear tape.

2. Cut a long length of mason line and tightly wrap the seam.

3. After wrapping for about ¾", place the ball chain on top of the two pieces of bungee cord and keep wrapping, placing the mason line in between each ball of the chain.

4. When you are about 1¼" from the end, cut off the ball chain and wrap the mason line tightly for another ¾" before cutting, gluing and tucking in the end of the line. The remaining loop completes the bracelet's closure.

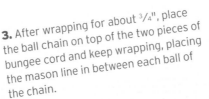

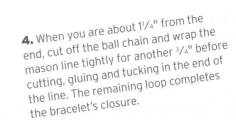

Tip

As a variation, you can wrap the mason line around every two balls of the chain, instead of just one. For even more sparkle, try replacing the ball chain with rhinestone chain: major bling guaranteed!

Three Finial Bangles

This is one of the easiest projects in this booklet, as it requires no clasp or closure, just a simple length of cord—a quarter inch thick or more—and a set of matching hex nut caps or simple finials, which can be found in the lighting department of a hardware store. The result is a classic bangle which looks best when worn on both arms and in multiples, all the way up to your elbow if you dare.

To Make Bangles

SKILL LEVEL
Beginner

CORD
One yard each of diamond braided polypropylene rope in the following diameters: ½", ⅜", and ¼".

NOTIONS
Scissors

Clear tape

Glue

Two finials or two hex nut caps to match the diameter of each rope (you can find these in any hardware store)

Cylindrical object around which to wrap your bangle

1. Cut the following lengths: 31" of the ½" dia. rope, 30½" of the ⅜" dia. rope and 29" of the ¼" dia. rope. Wrap the rope with a piece of clear tape before cutting to keep the fibers together. Secure both ends of the rope with a drop of glue to prevent fraying.

2. Put a few drops of glue into the hex nut cap (as shown above), or the finial of your choosing, and slip over the end of the rope. Hold firmly in place for at least a minute, then let dry for about 20 minutes. Do this for both ends of all three ropes.

3. One at a time, wrap each rope around your cylindrical mold, securing with little dabs of glue between the ropes as you go along. It's best to do this in small sections and hold the ropes together for at least a minute.

Finishing
Don't worry if your pieces ends up covered in glue threads, these can easily and safely be pulled off once your bangle is completely dry.

TIP

Look around your house and try to find just the right cylindrical mold for your bangle: It needs to be large enough to slip over your hand but not so large that it's always falling off. Here, a glass bottle ended up being too big, but a can of compressed air provided just the right diameter. Other candidates could be a rolling pin, or a cardboard mailing tube. If you pick the latter, make sure to wrap some heavy-duty packing or duct tape around your tube first, otherwise your bangle could end up being permanently glued to the cardboard tube.

Bead Bracelet

Sometimes the simplest of ideas are the most effective. The components of this bracelet are just that: three colorful strands showcasing a few plain wooden beads. There are no intricate designs, precious materials, or complicated techniques involved and yet . . . this will be the bracelet you will never want to take off!

SKILL LEVEL
Beginner

CORD
7" of elastic bungee cord 0.15" dia.

7" each of two colors parachute cord

Spool of nylon mason line

NOTIONS
Glue

Scissors

Clear tape

Three wooden beads

Bracelet clasp

Tip

Alternatives for the wooden beads could include plastic or papier-mâché beads, small brass hex nuts, tiny charms or rings. Do be careful not to choose anything too heavy, such as large glass beads, as it will make your bracelet "sag."

To Make Bracelet

1. Using a drop of glue, lightly dab the ends of the elastic bungee cord and both colors of parachute cord to prevent fraying. Cut a 40" length of mason line. Tape the three pieces of cord together with a small piece of clear tape.

2. Fold the mason line over in the middle and, starting from that middle point, wrap one end of your cord bundle tightly, leaving the other end to hang out. Once you have wrapped for about 1", cut off the mason line tail, glue the end and tuck under (you'll still have one mason line left to string beads on).

3. Take the other end of the mason line and string on a few beads, securing each bead into place by making a knot both before and after the bead.

4. Align beaded mason line with other cords, and tape the ends together. Use the mason line to wrap the other end of the bracelet tightly, starting at the end of the bracelet and working your way in. Once you have wrapped for about 1", cut off mason line, glue the end and tuck under.

5. Attach the clasp to both ends of the bracelet with a few drops of glue. Hold tightly into place for at least a minute, then let fully dry for about half an hour.

Friendship Bracelet

This bracelet's main feature is the strip of color(s), created by knotting embroidery floss in a technique very similar to a traditional blanket stitch. You can create a solid band of color, or a multi-hued striped pattern. The mercerized cotton of the embroidery floss will give your bracelet a beautiful lustrous appearance.

SKILL LEVEL
Beginner

CORD
One yard of elastic bungee cord 0.15" dia.

Embroidery floss

NOTIONS
Scissors

Glue

Two brass barrel couplings 3/8" dia. (these are plumbing fixtures you can find in any hardware store)

Clear tape

Tip

Try using two differently colored cords to make a thicker, brighter bracelet. Just follow the step but use two cords instead of one. Once you get to Step 4, use larger brass pieces and slide them over the mason line. Secure with a dab of glue on each side and enjoy!

To Make Bracelet

1. Cut a 27" piece of elastic bungee cord and fix both ends with a drop of glue to prevent fraying. Slip the cord twice through both barrel couplings.

2. Firmly tape both ends together, along with the rest of the cord. An added dollop of glue on this joint before taping will make it even more secure.

3. Cut 30" of embroidery floss and tie firmly with a double knot on the left side of the taped area. Loop the long length of the floss over the back, under the cords, back to the front and finally through the loop before tightening.

4. Keep repeating this process, making sure that you push the strands of the floss tightly and neatly together as you knot—no bungee cords should be visible underneath. Every once in a while, you may also need to straighten the row of knots you are creating on top. Once you have covered the entire length of the seam, cut off the floss and tuck the end underneath.

5. Finally, slip the barrel couplings in place over each end of the floss with a small dab of glue. Done!

Charm Bracelet

Believe it or not, charm bracelets have been around since prehistoric times. It seems that we have always had a need to decorate our wrists with trinkets that have personal significance to us. Whether the charms are simple shells or precious gems, the bracelet is always an expression of our personality. The charms remind us of certain times and places, and most importantly, of the people in our lives.

SKILL LEVEL
Intermediate

CORD
One yard of elastic bungee cord 0.15" dia.

Spool of mason line in various colors

NOTIONS
Scissors

Glue

Aluminum cable ferrule 3/16" dia. (this is a plumbing fixture you can find in any hardware store)

Clear tape

Two or three 0.94" split rings

To Make Bracelet

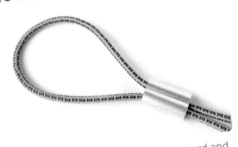

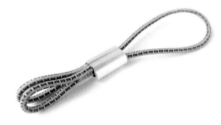

1. Cut a 21" piece of elastic bungee cord and fix both ends with a drop of glue to prevent fraying. Slip on cable ferrule and determine the right size of the bracelet by slipping it over your wrist. Secure the ferrule in place by slipping it over a small dab of glue and by taping a piece of clear tape right below it.

2. Cut the two remaining ends of bungee cord to a length of 4" and fix both ends with a drop of glue to prevent fraying. Fold both ends over towards the cable ferrule and secure in place with a dab of glue and a piece of clear tape.

3. Cut a long length of mason line and start wrapping all 4 pieces of bungee cord together. After about half an inch, continue wrapping just the loop. Once the entire loop is wrapped, cut off the mason line, tuck under the end and secure with a dab of glue.

4. Slip two or three split rings onto the loop. Wrap a length of mason line about 20 times around a piece of folded-up paper that is about 2½" long. Cut through one end of the mason-yarn bundle and slip it though a split ring.

5. Tie off the bundle underneath with a contrasting color of mason line and tuck in the end. Give your small tassel a "haircut" and finally fix each individual strand with a dab of glue to prevent fraying. Repeat this process for the other tassels.

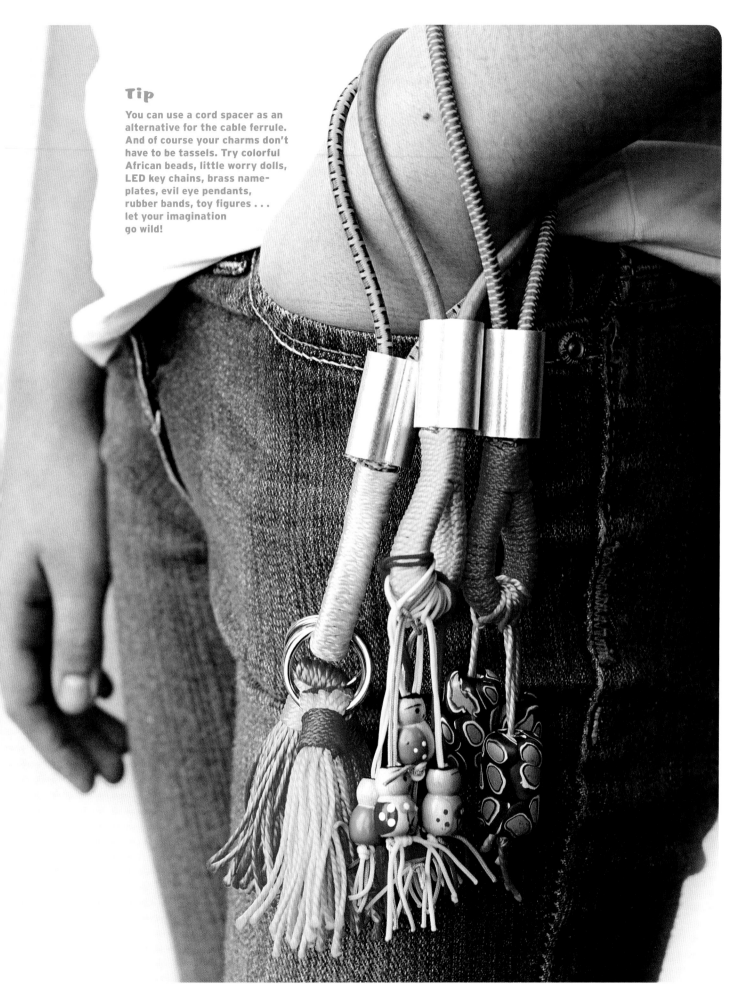

Tip

You can use a cord spacer as an alternative for the cable ferrule. And of course your charms don't have to be tassels. Try colorful African beads, little worry dolls, LED key chains, brass name-plates, evil eye pendants, rubber bands, toy figures . . . let your imagination go wild!

15

Brass Pipe Bracelet

The hardware store is a wonderfully inspiring place to hunt for supplies to make your bungee jewelry extra special and unique. Case in point are these brass pipe nipples (yes, that is in fact the correct term for these), which elevate this bungee cuff bracelet to a true fashion-forward statement piece and conversation starter.

To Make Bracelet

SKILL LEVEL
Intermediate

CORD
One yard each of two colors elastic bungee cord 0.15" dia.

Mason line

NOTIONS
Scissors

Glue

Two brass pipe nipples 1/8" dia. X smallest length*

Two brass pipe nipples 1/8" dia. X 2" long*

Clear tape

One carabiner closure 1 1/2" long

* (these are plumbing fixtures you can find in any hardware store)

1. Cut a 25" piece of each elastic bungee cord color and fix both ends with a drop of glue to prevent fraying.

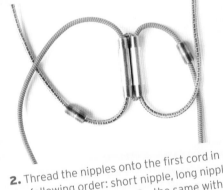

2. Thread the nipples onto the first cord in the following order: short nipple, long nipple, long nipple, short nipple. Do the same with the second cord, but in a reverse direction, starting with the other end of the short nipple.

3. Pull the cords tight with the nipples gathered in the middle. Lay the bracelet flat and cut off the ends on both sides at a length of 4 1/2" (starting measurement at the short brass nipple). Tape both cords together and fold over by 1 1/2". Secure with a dab of glue and another piece of tape. Repeat this step for the other end.

4. Wrap both ends with a length of mason line, leaving a half inch loop on either side. Fix the end of the mason line with a drop of glue and tuck under the end. Finally, clip on the carabiner for closure.

Tip

You can increase
the size and
amount of brass
for an even
bolder look.

Nautical Bracelet

This chic little bracelet uses a Josephine or "pretzel" knot to great effect. This is a classic sailor's knot, named after Empress Josephine, who was renowned for her trendsetting style. The Josephine knot—also known as a lover's knot—intertwines two separate strands to make the whole pattern. What better reason to make these bracelets as gifts or valentines?

SKILL LEVEL
Beginner

CORD
One yard each of two colors diamond braided polypropylene rope ¼" dia.

Mason line

NOTIONS
Scissors

Glue

Clear tape

Cylindrical object around which to wrap your bangle

Tip

Once you have mastered the simple Josephine knot, try going for a double, or even a triple version: once you've laid out a loose version of the knot, insert another length—or two—of cord to follow the path of the first cord, and do this with both colors. When tightening the knot, make sure to keep the whole thing neat and flat.

To Make Bracelet

1. Cut two 20" lengths of polypropylene rope, one in each color, and fix the ends with a drop of glue to prevent fraying. Intertwine both pieces into a Josephine knot—follow the picture above for guidance.

2. Gently tighten the knot until snug.

3. Tape both pieces of rope at either end together with clear tape.

4. Wrap bracelet around a mold—in this case a can of compressed air—and stick the overlapping ends together with a dollop of glue. Hold firmly in place for at least a minute.

5. Secure this seam by tightly wrapping a length of mason line around both layers. Glue and tuck under the ends.

Half + Half Bracelet

A super-simple design that showcases the beauty and colors of the various bungee cords, and allows for an infinite number of color combinations. This is yet another bracelet that takes mere minutes to make, and looks best when worn in multiples, and layered with other wrist candy for a truly original look.

To Make Bracelet

SKILL LEVEL
Beginner

CORD
Quarter of a yard each of two colors elastic bungee cord 0.15" dia.

NOTIONS
Scissors

Glue

Spring coils to fit the diameter of the bungee cord, with and without lobster closures

Pliers

1. Cut a 8" piece of both colors elastic bungee cord and fix both ends with a drop of glue to prevent fraying.

2. Link both cords to each other in the middle, using a lanyard knot.

3. Slip a simple spring coil over each of the cord ends on one side, securing the coil to the cord by clamping down the last wire with a pair of pliers.

4. Slip a spring coil with a lobster closure over each of the two cord ends on the other side, securing the coil to the cord by clamping down the last wire with a pair of pliers. Done!

Tip

You can double up on the bungee cord to make a more substantial bracelet, as long as you select the spring coil size to accommodate the diameters of both cords.

copper Necklace

Forget about old and silver, copper is trending as the chic new metal color. It is both cool and contemporary, yet warm and earthy. Wearing copper jewelry is an age-old folk remedy for promoting a healthy immune system. True or not, copper is cool, especially when combined with like-minded shades of red, hot pink, and orange.

To Make Necklace

SKILL LEVEL
Beginner

CORD
Two yards each of two colors nylon parachute cord 5/32" dia. (red and hot pink)

Two yards each of two colors elastic bungee cord 0.15" dia. (light pink and orange)

Two yards of diamond braided polypropylene rope ¼" dia. (orange/reflective)

NOTIONS
Scissors

Glue

Clear tape

Two copper couplings ³/8" dia.*

One copper adapter ³/4" dia. X 1½" long*

One box of copper crimp sleeves gauge 18-10

Pliers

*(these are plumbing fixtures you can find in any hardware store)

1. Cut a 45" length of both parachute cords, both bungee cords, and the rope, and fix the ends with a drop of glue to prevent fraying.

2. Temporarily tape both ends of this bundle together in order to push them through the copper couplings. There should be a coupling at each end.

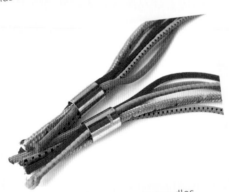

3. Remove tape, gather both bundles and now tape all twelve pieces together in order to push this new bundle through the adapter.

4. Pull cords and ropes through the adapter until about 5" is sticking out underneath. Insert a copper crimp sleeve over the end of each cord and flatten with pliers.

22

Tip

This long necklace is so fast to make, you will not want to stop at just one: Experiment with the colors and gauge of the cord and with the configuration of the copper fixtures, or try knotting your bundle in between two pieces of copper couplings before joining both ends into the copper adapter.

Bib Necklace

The bright Day-Glo colors of the nylon diamond braided ropes in this necklace evoke the semi-precious stones and enamels used in ancient Egyptian bib necklaces. Also called the breast-plate necklace, the bib is a fun and flattering statement piece for a 21st-century Cleopatra: boldly colored and daring in style.

SKILL LEVEL
Intermediate

CORD
One yard each of the diamond braided polypropylene rope ¼" dia. in blue/white and blue/grey

Half a yard of diamond braided polypropylene rope ¼" dia. (orange/reflective)

One yard of diamond braided polypropylene rope 3/16" dia. (pink/white)

Half a yard of diamond braided polypropylene rope ½" dia. (blue/black)

Spool of mason line in pink

Spool of mason line in orange

NOTIONS
Scissors

Glue

Two 3/16" cable stops*

One S-biner closure

One brass pipe nipple 3/8" dia., 2" long*

Four silver hex nuts 5/16"*

* (found in hardware stores)

Tip
Considering the many components and joints for this type of necklace, it is crucial to cut out all the components beforehand and lay them out on your work surface. Infinite variations are possible here, enjoy!

To Make Necklace

1. Cut a 26" piece of the blue/white rope and fix the ends with a drop of glue to prevent the yarns from fraying. Slip on two cable stops.

2. Fold over both ends by about 3" and glue in place for 2" only, leaving a 1" loop on either side. Wrap mason line in 2 colors around both ends, tuck in ends and secure with a drop of glue (described in "Basic Techniques" on page 4). Push cable stops right up to wrapped section. Clip on S-biner as closure between both loops.

3. Cut 12" piece of ½" dia. blue/black rope and fix the ends with a drop of glue. Center this piece underneath the blue/white necklace and glue together with small dabs of glue. This completes the top part of the necklace.

4. For the bottom part, cut an 8" piece of orange/reflective rope and a 15" piece of blue/grey rope, and fix all ends with glue. Slip the brass nipple onto the orange/reflective rope and center below the blue/grey rope. Position in place with a few dabs of glue. Wrap pink mason line over both joints, tuck in ends and secure with a drop of glue. Slip two hex nuts over either end of the bottom necklace.

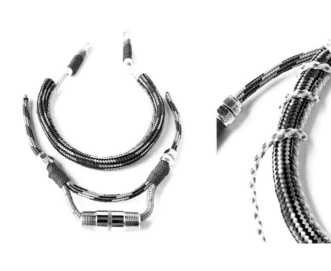

5. Glue both ends of the bottom necklace to the sides of the top necklace. Wrap pink/white rope over the left joint—holding together 3 ropes—and after 6 turns, keep wrapping in a spiral fashion, securing with little dabs of glue as you go along, but only over the blue/white and blue/black ropes. Finally, wrap over entire right joint 6 times, tuck under end and secure with a small dab of glue.

Wired Necklace

Beauty and inspiration can be found in the strangest places. Have you ever seen the insides of those big optical fiber cables that traverse oceans and span hundreds of thousands of kilometers? This necklace is an tongue-in-cheek homage to the beauty of technology, exposed for the world to see. The mix and match of colors, patterns, and gauges makes this a truly customizable piece.

SKILL LEVEL
Beginner

CORD
Half a yard of heavy duty diamond braided polypropylene rope ¼" dia. (this will be the core necklace)

One yard each of various colors diamond braided polypropylene rope ³/₁₆" dia. and ¼" dia.

One yard each of various colors nylon parachute cord ⁵/₃₂" dia.

NOTIONS
Scissors

Glue

Metal bracelet closure

Drapery clip rings 1¼" dia.

Pliers

Clear tape

Clear duct tape

Tip

Finishing can be tricky! For added strength, secure the cords with a dab of glue *before* taping to ensure that your necklace will hold!

To Make Necklace

1. Cut an 18" length from your heavy duty rope, and fix both ends with a drop of glue to prevent fraying. Put a few drops of glue into both ends of the metal closure and insert ends of core necklace. Hold firmly in place for at least a minute, then let dry for about 20 minutes.

2. Cut 28" lengths in various colors from all your other ropes: The necklace pictured here features 6 pieces of ¼" dia. (including one color which is glow-in-the-dark), 2 pieces of ³/₁₆" dia. and 6 lengths of parachute cord. Secure all ends with a drop of glue.

3. Clip on the drapery rings all around the core necklace at equal distance from each other. Bend the rings with pliers so that they hang perpendicular to the clip (rather than parallel with the clip).

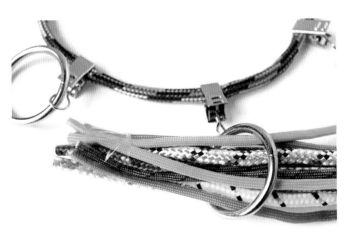

4. Lightly tape all the 28" lengths of rope together into a bundle in order to thread them through the drapery rings. Remove the tape from the bundle.

5. Next, use clear duct tape to connect each individual cord to its opposite end at the back of the necklace. You will only need to open the closure on the core necklace in order to fit the necklace over your head. Major fashion statement guaranteed!

Sunburst Necklace

This necklace takes its style cues from the radiant and celestial sunburst mirror. The design of this iconic mirror may hark all the way back to 17th century France, the era of King Louis XIV, also known as the Sun King. Whatever its beginnings may be, the sunburst is a timeless design that makes the most flattering frame for your face.

SKILL LEVEL
Intermediate

CORD

One yard of diamond braided polypropylene rope ¼" dia. (for the core yellow/black necklace)

One yard of diamond braided polypropylene rope ¼" dia. (orange/reflective)

Two and a half yards of diamond braided polypropylene rope ¼" dia. (white/red/black)

Three and a half yards of diamond braided polypropylene rope ³/₁₆" dia. (yellow/green/black)

Five yards of nylon parachute cord (fluorescent yellow)

Spools of mason line in various colors (yellow, fluorescent yellow, and orange)

NOTIONS

Scissors

Glue

Bracelet clasp 1¼" long*

Silver hex nuts ⁵/₁₆"*

Brass hex nuts #10*

* (found in hardware stores)

Tip

Consider using large glass or African beads instead of hex nuts for a more exotic look. You can also up the drama factor by knotting alternating shorter and much longer ends onto the core necklace. Make the core necklace much longer for a finished piece that will take on the allure of decorative fringe from the 1920s.

To Make Necklace

1. Cut a 19" piece of ¼" dia. yellow/black rope for the core necklace and fix both ends with a drop of glue. Thread one end through the hole in the clasp, fold over by 1 inch and secure with a dab of glue. Fold over the other end by 1½" and secure 1" with a dab of glue, leaving a half inch loop. Secure both ends by wrapping around yellow mason line, tuck in ends and attach with a little more glue.

2. Cut 20" pieces in the following quantities: 1 orange/reflective (OR), 4 white/red/black (WRB), 6 yellow/green/black (YGB) and 8 fluorescent yellow parachute cord (FLY). Tie all the pieces to the core necklace, using a lanyard knot, as seen in the picture. The color layout is, from left to right: YGB, FLY (double up on cord), YGB, WRB, FLY (double up on cord), WRB, YGB, OR, YGB, WRB, FLY (double up on cord), WRB, YGB, FLY (double up on cord), YGB.

3. Slip one silver hex nut on each of the diamond braided rope ends except for the orange/reflective rope in the middle that gets three silver hex nuts. Slip one brass hex nut on each of the yellow parachute cord ends. Lay the necklace flat and trim the various ends to the desired size, from 4½" in the middle to 3½" at the sides of the necklace. Fix all the ends with glue.

4. Finish all the diamond rope ends by wrapping mason line underneath the hex nut and all the way to the end, tucking in ends and gluing again.

5. Finish the parachute cord ends by wrapping and double knotting a short end of mason line under each hex nut. Trim the tails of the mason line. Using a little glue, secure the knot to create a bead that holds the hex nut in place.

Resources

A.C. Moore
Arts & Crafts superstores in the eastern United States from Maine to Florida.
www.acmoore.com

Beverly Fabrics
Craft and fabric store selling online and in retail shops throughout California
www.beverlys.com

Hancock Fabrics^{SM}
Fabrics, craft & jewelry supplies
www.hancockfabrics.com

Hobby Lobby®
Retailer for arts and crafts supplies, both online and with over 500 store locations.
www.hobbylobby.com

Home Depot®
Hardware and home improvement centers
www.homedepot.com

Jo-Ann®
Fabric and craft stores
www.joann.com

Michaels®
North America's largest specialty retailer of arts and crafts for the hobbyist.
www.michaels.com

Pepperell
Manufacturer of bungee cords and bungee accessories
www.pepperell.com

www.bungeecentral.com
Supplier of a variety bungee cord and accessories

www.parachutecordcraft.com
Parachute cords and all related accessories in an online store

www.save-on-crafts.com
A crafting site for do-it-yourselfers on a budget.

f you like these projects, you'll love these other fun craft booklets:

DecoDen Bling
Mini decorations for phones & favorite things

Alice Fisher

DecoDen is all about bringing bling to every aspect of your life—from your sunglasses to your cellphone to everything in between! Best of all, the decadent sparkle of this hot decorating technique is just a few simple techniques away. From phone cases to wall clocks to picture frames and more, the 20 recipes in this booklet will show you exactly what you need to glam up your day.

32 pages, product #078046, $9.95 U.S.

Arm Knitting
chunky cowls, scarves, and other no-needle knits

Linda Zemba Burhance

Knitting your own scarf, cowl, or blanket is easier than you think, and with the brilliant new technique called arm knitting, it couldn't be quicker. Each of these 12 projects knit up in under an hour and only require a few skeins of yarn. Best of all, you don't need any tools—just bring your arms and hands! Go wild with the bright colors of the Fun Times Scarf, add a sophisticated layer to your date night outfit with the Evening Sparkle Tie-on Shrug, or just cuddle up with the Super Cozy Throw. Just know that your friends are going to want some of their own!

32 pages, product #078045, $9.95 U.S.

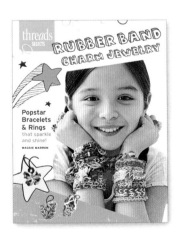

Rubber Band Charm Jewelry
popstar bracelets & rings that sparkle and shine

Maggie Marron

This booklet offers 15 great jewelry projects to make on or off of your loom—rings, bracelets, anklets, and even charms made out of nothing but rubber bands! Spice up your day the popstar way and let loose with these celebrity-inspired accessories. Learn how to make fishtails, starbursts, tulips, and so much more as you grab a little piece of the spotlight for yourself!

32 pages, product #078047, $9.95 U.S.

Shop for these and other great craft books and booklets online: www.tauntonstore.com

Simply search by product number or call 800-888-8286, use code MX800126

Call Monday-Friday 9AM - 9PM EST and Saturday 9AM - 5PM EST • International customers, call 203-702-2204

Look for these other *Threads* Selects booklets at www.tauntonstore.com and wherever crafts are sold.

Prairie Girl Gifts
EAN: 9781621139492
8 ½ x 10 ⅞, 32 pages
Product# 078030
$9.95 U.S., $9.95 Can.

Pet Projects to Knit
EAN: 9781627100991
8 ½ x 10 ⅞, 32 pages
Product# 078034
$9.95 U.S., $9.95 Can.

Cute Pets to Knit
EAN: 9781627107747
8 ½ x 10 ⅞, 32 pages
Product# 078043
$9.95 U.S., $9.95 Can.

Button Jewelry
EAN: 9781627107808
8 ½ x 10 ⅞, 32 pages
Product# 078040
$9.95 U.S., $9.95 Can.

Bead Necklaces
EAN: 9781621137641
8 ½ x 10 ⅞, 32 pages
Product# 078002
$9.95 U.S., $9.95 Can.

Drop Earrings
EAN: 9781621137658
8 ½ x 10 ⅞, 32 pages
Product# 078003
$9.95 U.S., $9.95 Can.

Bead Bracelets
EAN: 9781621139515
8 ½ x 10 ⅞, 32 pages
Product# 078028
$9.95 U.S., $9.95 Can.

Crocheted Hearts & Flowers
EAN: 9781627107761
8 ½ x 10 ⅞, 32 pages
Product# 078044
$9.95 U.S., $9.95 Can.

Easy-to-Sew Flowers
EAN: 9781621138259
8 ½ x 10 ⅞, 32 pages
Product# 078017
$9.95 U.S., $9.95 Can.

Easy-to-Sew Tote Bags
EAN: 9781621138297
8 ½ x 10 ⅞, 32 pages
Product# 078021
$9.95 U.S., $9.95 Can.

Easy-to-Sew Gifts
EAN: 9781621138310
8 ½ x 10 ⅞, 32 pages
Product# 078023
$9.95 U.S., $9.95 Can.

Beaded Gifts
EAN: 9781627107730
8 ½ x 10 ⅞, 32 pages
Product# 078039
$9.95 U.S., $9.95 Can.